55+ Unite!

Welcome All Wise, Working Women

Georgian Lussier

ISBN-10: 1466411120
ISBN-13: 978-1466411128

DEDICATION

This book is an open love letter to all women who busted down doors and now feel locked out. Finding ways to earn money when the world sees you as a crone can be grueling. Fortunately, you have post-menopausal zest and faithful friends in your arsenal. Don't buy into aging myths: Summon all the strengths and spirit that got you this far. And in the words of Mark Twain, "wrinkles should merely indicate where the smiles have been."

Best Regards,
Georgian Lussier
Age 61

Never say Never!

Georgian

01/12

X

CONTENTS

ACKNOWLEDGMENTS

Thank you to Sue Raggo, Linda Herrmann and Jan Hecht, who generously brought their brilliant mid-life brains to this topic. Jan also did a superlative editing job on this book; any mistakes are mine.

Also, thanks to my daughter for sharing her marketing skills and ideas.

Please take note of my recommended readings – there is a sample of inspirational and informative contributions by women writers.

Georgian Lussier

Chapter 1. We've Got the Power: Let's Help Each Other

> *Our middle-aged brains are surprisingly competent and surprisingly talented. We're smarter, calmer, happier, and as one scientist, herself in middle age, put it: "We just know stuff."*
>
> Barbara Strauch,
> *The Secret Life of the Grown-Up Brain*

Remember Betty Boop, the animated 30s flapper who was flirty, flighty and full of fun? With a wink and a giggle, she cavorted from one near calamity to another. She portrayed an early example of sexual harassment in the workplace when her circus-performing character pleaded with her manager

1

"Don't take my boop-oop-a-doop away!" (She was rescued by her guy in the nick of time.) Betty was a tangy tonic for downtrodden women who lived in a man's world.

Forty years later, America was graced by Betty Ford. While her marriage to Jerry was initially postponed over concerns about how voters would react to his marrying a "divorced ex-dancer," Betty brought a breath of fresh air to the White House. She sallied forth on controversial topics, such as sex, drugs and gun control. She used her battles with breast cancer and alcoholism to inspire others, and became tremendously popular with the public. One slogan said, "Vote for Betty's Husband." Betty Ford supported the ERA when the women's movement was flush with promise and passion. When she died at age 93, she was heralded as someone who liberated us all from labels. Her daughter continues her legacy at the famous Betty Ford Center.

Fast-forward another forty years, to our present time
— and — ta-da! – Betty White! Whew, she's 89, has
64 years of television experience and recently won the
Screen Actors Guild Award for best female actor in a
comedy series. Betty is credited with a Midwestern
work ethic, but is far from a prude. Somewhat like
Betty Boop, she uses sexual innuendoes to entertain.
But that is where the resemblance ends. In her latest
book, *If You Ask Me: (And of Course You Won't),* she
offers a sobering assessment of working mothers: "I
know there are many career girls today who would
disagree, but I'm not a big believer in being able to do
both. I think somebody takes the short end of the
stick." All working moms know there are no easy
answers, and despite the legal battles won by our
sisters in the '70s, kids and careers can be evil twins.

Career Crones?

Unless we are raising our grandchildren, 55+ women
have traded the kid/career dilemma for a new duality:
credentials/opportunities. Despite graduate degrees,
mounds of management experience and finely honed
skills, women over 55 are off the employment grid.

3

Who wants to hire a crone when the market is awash with talent that is toned, tanned and far from the twilight years? Besides, aren't older women all set?

In our jobless recovery, it's easy to pass over the women who were inspired by Betty Friedan. Our hearts readily go out to the recent grads with $25,000 in school loans; to the young couples who have to uproot their families in search of a job; to the single moms with three part-time jobs and no benefits. To the unemployed dads who awkwardly wait at school bus stops.

Aging professional women are encouraged to spend their final career chapter in low-paying or no-paying charity jobs — to give back to the community and maybe rediscover some artistic skills or smoldering life goals. Nice gig, if you can afford it. But despite years of career success, many 55+ women are running out of gas. Houses are underwater, health benefits are unaffordable and husbands are hamstrung. A cadre of capable older women need a job, want to work and come with street credibility.

As with any generalizations, there are exceptions. Some women over 55 always snagged a chair before the reorganizational music stopped. Others were especially frugal, stayed in unfulfilling jobs with security or are still extremely successful in their chosen paths. Some *do* have husbands who provide a comfortable, retired lifestyle. But many women who broke sound barriers in the workplace need to keep working.

Older women cannot wait for social reform to address their employment conundrum. With each year of the poor economy, we get older and less visible in the job market. This book is a call-to-arms: As aging women, we need to leverage our strengths, face down our fears and prop one another up.

The Good News: Five Positive Findings About 55+

There is no greater power in the world than the zest of postmenopausal women

Margaret Mead

1. Our Brain Power

Our middle-aged, female brains are wired for continued success. True, we are sometimes held hostage by a stubborn word that shall not be retrieved — until it is no longer needed, and then it pops out. And we carry a list to remember what we need from the basement. But emerging brain research says that is only part of the story.

Barbara Strauch's terrific book, *The Secret Life of the Grown-Up Brain*, cites research that suggests our propensity for making connections is strengthened with age and experience. We get better at sizing up situations, recognizing patterns, making good decisions, anticipating consequences and overcoming obstacles. Without breaking a sweat, we weave creative solutions out of seemingly disparate pieces. While our processing speed is slower, our results are profound.

In a *New York Times* article about the announcement that the legendary basketball coach, Pat Summitt, has early-stage Alzheimer's, an expert made an interesting computer analogy. Dr. Gary Kennedy, the director of geriatric psychiatry at Montefiore Medical Center in the Bronx, said Summitt's good health and history of high achievement works in her favor. "Everyone's processor slows down as we age, but we compensate with our experience. We get better at recognizing patterns, and that makes up for the loss of speed. In other words, our hardware slows down, but we upgrade our software." (NYT, "Unfamiliar Path Unfolds At Tennessee," by Lynn Zinser - 08/31/11)

2. Our Thinking Style

In her book, *The First Sex*, Helen Fisher offers a historical and anthropological perspective on women through the ages. The title refers to the fact that embryos start out asexual; around week eight, hormones may start producing a boy. If not, a female begins to flourish. Taking umbrage with scientists who refer to women as "the default plan," Fisher prefers to think of women as the primary, or first, sex.

Fisher's book covers a lot of territory, but I found her section on how women think to be especially relevant for those of us who are 55+. Subtitled "The Natural

Talents of Women And How They Are Changing the World," the book posits that women are "web thinkers." Fisher believes that women's tendency to think contextually and holistically, while exercising a lot of flexibility, intuition and imagination, gives us a boost in the business world. Our natural ability to think in interrelated ways helps us focus on process, as well as results. This kind of system thinking is touted by Peter Senge, author of the business bible, *The Fifth Discipline.*

Given that our brains only get better at recognizing patterns and drawing on many factors to make decisions as we age, our systems thinking skills are especially keen in mid-life.

3. Our Wisdom

While age does not guarantee wisdom, women past 55 are likely at their peak capacity for making wise decisions. Theorists are far from agreeing on the essence of wisdom, but there are some common qualities that appear in the research. As reported by Stephen S. Hall in *The New York Times Magazine* on

May 6, 2011, wisdom is thought to include emotional resiliency; the ability to cope in the face of adversity; a clear-eyed view of human nature and the human predicament; openness to other possibilities; and a knack for learning from lifetime experiences. Generosity, vs. an occupation with self, is also associated with wisdom. Oh, and humility and forgiveness.

The same *New York Times* article references the Berlin Wisdom Paradigm, as well as a Three Dimensional Wisdom Scale questionnaire that is available on the NYT site. In *The Secret Life of the Grown-Up Brain*, Barbara Stauch cites Elkhonon Goldberg's book, *The Wisdom Paradox.* A professor of neurology, Goldberg believes his own mid-life brain had developed a kind of "mental magic." He suggests that his increased, instantaneous insight may be "perchance that coveted attribute … wisdom?"

My guess is that none of us would claim to be all-knowing or wondrously wise. However, consider this: We are assuredly wiser than when we were young, and our experience offers us a solid base for navigating challenges with aplomb. Embedded in our state-of-the-art mental software, wisdom and web thinking make us a formidable force in the business world.

4. Our Strength in Numbers

Helen Fisher, author of *The First Sex*, believes that at middle age we get a "dividend from nature." As our estrogen declines, testosterone and other androgens are unmasked. This is associated with an increase in assertiveness and independence in middle-aged women, as witnessed around the world. Factor in the number of baby-boomer women, and you can appreciate why historian Gerda Lerner is quoted in Fisher's book as proclaiming that "Such a critical mass of older women with a tradition of rebellion and independence and a way of making a living has not occurred before in history."

In 2011, I participated in a webinar and learned that there are approximately 50 million American women aged 50 and above. This group has significant influence within families; they are credited with making 80% of all buying decisions, and 65% of health decisions. Baby boomers also spend the most money among all women and are active on Facebook, with friends and family. As our economy is dependent on consumer confidence, it would benefit all of America if we were more acknowledged in this youth-oriented culture.

From a social work perspective, older women are connectors and networkers who share their wisdom and look for support. We seek recommendations from people we trust, and value transparency. One third of women 51–64 are considered to be in the "sandwich generation"; they have responsibilities for both children and parents. The typical "Alpha Daughter" is age 60 and coordinates care for her 85-year-old mother. Still, in the media, older women remain relatively invisible.

Millions of women age 55+ are educated, experienced and assertive. Surely we can help one another become more of a visible, vibrant force in the workplace, as well as the retail market.

5. Our Fierce Friendships

While we are growing wise we forge rich friendships with other women. In a *USA Today* article by Mary Brophy, clinical psychologist Samantha Litzinger said, "Creating a bond with other women creates a rich space in our lives. Women need other women to feel creative with, to laugh with, and explore life with. There's a certain freedom that can bloom in later-life friendships between women. It's that sense of 'We're in this together.' "

(USA Today - 6/21/11)

Betty White, in her latest book, *If You Ask Me: (And of Course You Won't),* reminds us that friendships wilt when neglected. She urges us to not get so comfortable that we take our friends for granted. Her books are filled with unabashed fondness and love for many friends, including animals, who have added to her long and colorful life.

In *The First Sex*, Helen Fisher proposes that ancestral women formed sisterly coalitions to increase their chances for survival and protection, thereby ensuring a future generation. She also credits estrogen with driving women to form harmonious, egalitarian relationships with one another.

I suspect we do not need to be convinced of the benefits of having good girlfriends. However, I suggest that when it comes to our 55+ dilemma, we should consider them as secret weapons. Most women have much deeper friendships than men do. Since we are at risk of being invisible and under-appreciated, we need to fight for one another. Time is not on our side, and we need to act with a sense of urgency. As Seneca said back in the Roman days, "While we are postponing, life speeds by."

Food for Thought:
Trials and Triumphs at 55+

In the following chapters, I share my own story of working past 55, highlight career timelines of some of my 55+ associates, and invite you to sketch your own career profile. Using a few of my friendships as examples, I remind us all to treasure the power of sisterhood — sometimes all it takes is one woman telling another that she still has a lot to offer.

On a more spiritual level, I end with a lucky Las Vegas story, and honor the companionship of two perfectly precious Portuguese Pointers. Included is a compassionate tale about Pokey, a rescue cat who has become a sergeant-at-arms. As the veterinarian who donated some of her services for this tiny, sick kitten said, "What if the Hokey Pokey is really what it's all about?"

Chapter 2. Duped at 58!

Losing my job at age 58 was a wretched affair.
Ambushed under the pretense of a regular meeting, I
was told my job was eliminated, and that a security
official would watch me as I packed up my things —
immediately. No, it was not performance related —
just a business decision. Back in my office, I
summoned my most professional self as I put my
many management books in a box that advertised
adult diapers.

I had accepted this job after a whirlwind courtship ten
months earlier. Luckily, thirty years of experience
taught me that corporate life is, indeed, fickle — and
it's never just about you. But there was a new wrinkle
in this scenario — I was now an older worker, and a
woman, to boot. Unbeknownst to me at the time, I
was in danger of becoming invisible.

****

I know people are supposed to get more rigid as they age, but my most important decisions have been heart over head – and my heart doesn't know how old it is. I surprised myself by getting married at 22 and by becoming a mother at 37. When I divorced my corporate life at age 44 to become an independent consultant, I did not envision a return engagement.

But when I was 57, a company I was consulting with fell in love with me. I was wearing my "compensation" hat, which includes salary surveys, job evaluation and position descriptions. With minimal effort, I created a dog-and-pony show about pay equity and administration. The content was basic to me but new to this management group. As the managers and supervisors were in locations throughout the state, I gave the same presentation many times.

I injected a little humor as I talked about the company's pay levels and practices. Using an ancient compensation analogy, one slide showed a jar of peanut butter and a piece of bread – the point being, spreading pay increases evenly across a company does little to recognize high performance and encourages an entitlement mentality. I breezed through these presentations and effectively engaged my audiences. I was a star!

It was easy to resist an invitation to apply for a permanent compensation job with this company; I had thirty years of experience in the field – been there, done that. And despite the roller-coaster ride of being self-employed, I loved the independence. But a job opening for an organizational development director was seductive; leading groups, training managers and orchestrating new programs makes my heart go pitty-pat.

So, at 58, I started a full-time job, after 14 years of consulting. The work was exciting, I knew the management team, the commute was short, and the pay was in line with my experience and education. What could go wrong?

Another reason I gave up my business was more personal; my Dad had died recently, around the time my daughter miraculously survived a life-threatening accident. While it was a radical change to leave my consulting practice, I was jarred by the turbulence in my home life, and everything seemed up for grabs.

In retrospect, it was somewhat remarkable to leap back into a corporate job at 58. At the time, my age was not a feature in my decision. I had no plans to retire and felt at the top of my game. In addition, my boss and counterpart were also newly hired women over 50. We were a small team of highly skilled professionals: Age and experience gave us the credibility needed to introduce cultural change.

But within a year, the 2008 economic crash catapulted me onto my front porch. I was not the only one – a fistful of us were ejected, all women over 50 earning good pay and benefits. Additional pruning within the company affected men and women of all ages, but I suspect some were relieved to be rid of the HR crones. The bloom was definitely off the rose.

I swung through the stages of loss relatively gracefully– shock and denial morphed into acceptance faster than it would have in my younger days. But I did feel tricked – by the company that hired me, as well as myself. Why did I keep falling for the idea that everyone wants a more open workplace? I felt like one of those women who complain about men in advice columns, only to be told they subconsciously date guys afraid of commitment.

But I could not afford to indulge in feeling sorry for myself. As Mary Pickford said, "If you have made mistakes, there is always another chance for you. You may have a fresh start any moment you choose. For this thing we call 'failure' is not the falling down, but the staying down." I had to stay focused on getting up.

My first instinct was to resurrect my consulting practice. I needed to dust off my files and make some magic. Damn! My business insurance was lapsed, my web site disabled, my contacts outdated. Right away, I created postcard-sized announcements to let people know I was back in business.

The effects of being booted out still stung – I was disenchanted with the politics of full-time employment, but reminded myself to stay open to all possibilities. So I put on my big-girl pants and got on with it.

The Incredibly Shrinking Woman

Fortunately, my pants were not as big as they used to be. One gift I had recently given myself was membership in a weight-loss group at work. I'm short, and carried way too many pounds for way too many years. At first, I did not want to publicize my weight problems in my new job — but come on, did I really think it was a secret?

While I enjoy collaborating on creative projects, and facilitate groups in my consulting work, I couldn't picture myself a happy camper in a fat club. On initial impression, our leader struck me as chirpy — she was informal, expressive, and wore dresses that reminded me of *I Love Lucy*. To my delight, she quickly established herself as a caring, informed friend — the ultimate cheerleader, but someone who did not buy

excuses.   Week after week, she graciously hosted a
gathering based on acceptance and support.

At my first weekly weigh-in, I'd lost 4.5 pounds! I was
jolted into action. After tracking everything I ate for
seven months, and ingesting heaps of fiber but very
little sugar, I lost 40 pounds. My body shape shrank
back into proportion, and I felt healthier. Inside, I
was the same old me, but the reaction from others was
a kick. And what a thrill to swish around in last
summer's pants.

From my organizational development perspective, this
fat club had a great design. Members set individual
goals that they did not have to share with others. We
were supplied with strategies and tips for avoiding
forbidden foods at social events. Stickers and charms
rewarded interim results.

At each meeting, we shared stories, celebrated
successes and acknowledged setbacks. Our common
bond was our joint suffering — we formed an alliance
that transcended job titles. As the weekly weigh-in
approached, members in the cafeteria line would tease

one another about last-minute efforts to shave off a few ounces. The humor was wholesome, and we co-existed in a snark-free zone. Mean-girl behavior was off-limits.

This experience was positive on many levels for me, and I marveled at the willingness of women to share their struggles with people outside their immediate circles.

Wigged-Out

The blow of being dumped at work was buffered because I exerted less energy trying to hide my body. However, I exchanged one disguise for another — but this time I had more fun doing it. I started wearing wigs.

As I outwardly accepted my unemployment predicament, my inner self was freaking out, as in, my hair was falling out. One morning in the kitchen, my daughter was behind me and said, "Mom, you

know you are getting a bald spot in the back, right?"
Surprise!

Hair loss was not exactly new to me. Clumps had
come out after a car accident fueled by raging
hormones: My pregnant friend's husband drove us
into a very large tree. Teen mom and the baby were
okay, drunk dad was hospitalized, and my boyfriend
and I were dispatched to our parents. With youthful
exuberance, my hair grew back.

In another hair incident due to adolescent stupidity, I
bumped into a car as I entered a two-lane highway —
and the impact caused the passenger's wig to fly out
the window! I laughed *after* I called home to report
yet another fender bender. It took me a while to
appreciate how much attention is needed to drive
safely. Today, I am a "don't drive while distracted"
nag. Still, it was funny.

In the go-go '70s, I dyed my hair blond and
experimented with a long "fall" — remember those?
To conceal the "bump" where the combs attached at
my crown, I created a headband out of a psychedelic

scarf that is now back in style. Shades of Jersey
Shore, when you are in your 20s, you look good in
anything.

In my more mature years, I witnessed my
grandmother Angeline's hair loss. A French-Canadian
beauty, her once-magnificent mane abandoned her,
little by little, until she was left with baby chick fuzz.
She raised her family in Kansas, and her annual visits
to her daughters in Connecticut always included a trip
to Wig Town. One new wig a year kept her looking put
together until she died at 93.

Shortly before the market crashed and my job
disappeared, my Mom and I went to Wig Town, as
she's inherited Angeline's affliction. Mom is my
biggest fan, and insisted I get a wig, too: Her treat. I
agreed, as my fine hair wilts under a hint of wind, rain
or morning dew — defying the power of pricey hair
products.

My college-aged daughter was startled when I
appeared in my auburn bubble-cut. Had to admit, I
did resemble a member of one of those girl bands

from the early '60s. I nixed the idea of wearing it to work — it would cause a distraction from my very serious responsibilities. (Though not so serious that they couldn't soon do without me.)

Chance favors the prepared mind — or head, in my case. After I lost my job, I did not dwell on my hair loss; I was trying not to let anything blur my focus. I simply wore my wig whenever I left the house. That was three years ago, and I have since sported several wigs. Some are more flighty than others, but none can compare with that long, blond fall from my youth. Even though my hair grew back, I still rely on a wig to keep me looking put together, just like Grandma Angeline.

Being thinner, with a full head of beautiful fake hair, boosted my networking confidence. No one would mistake me as being young, but I looked much better than I did before I started a full-time job at 58. Not that I was thinking about my advanced age at 59 — that popped out as a 60th birthday present.

Glam Glasses

I'd been wearing sensible glasses for distance since my mid-20s. When I started having trouble reading the news stream at the bottom of the TV screen, I assumed my aging eyes had deteriorated. But time was on my side. The natural reshaping of my eyes helped me see better. Presented with a weaker prescription, I was so excited to have "younger" eyes that I spent $400 I didn't have on an edgy pair of sparkly black and white frames.

While I don't have buyer's remorse, a future option may be a glittery frame endorsed by Paula Deen, the food guru. Several celebrities have a line of eyeglasses, some available through Wal-Mart. The fact that many of them prefer contacts does not take away from the glamour of being associated with someone famous.

War Paint

While cosmetics cannot hide a turkey neck, airbrush makeup gives skin an even glow. An infomercial

promised a performance-ready sheen, and sharing the
system with my daughter helped justify the purchase.
While her kit of liquid foundation had shades of light,
opalescent coloring, mine matched my dark and
uneven hide. A daily ritual of spray-painting light
layers of base and bronzer created a protective barrier
against the glare of the working world.

Stacy and Clinton are the make-over experts. But I
know that "suddenly" being 60 requires a lot more
effort to stay in the game. Ultimately, though, exterior
fixes are superficial: As Lauren Bacall told us, "I think
your whole life shows in your face, and you should be
proud of that." So maybe the balancing act is to have
a sense of humor about your age, while taking
advantage of ways to prop up your professional image.

At some point, we all consider repair-and-overhaul
projects. Defying conventional wisdom about
avoiding elective surgery, some women in their 70s
and 80s opt for nips and tucks. In a *New York Times*
article by Abby Ellin on August 9, 2011, several
women of a certain age shared their stories of
banishing "slackened jowls, jiggly underarms and

saggy eyelids." Statistics show that over 84,000 people over age 65 had plastic surgery, and experts say some do so to look youthful in the world of work.

To me, the good news is that many women do what they think it takes to stay employed at 55+.

Having the rug pulled out from under you at age 55+ seems more onerous than at age 25.

But decades of experience can make us more open to possibilities and emotionally stable.

Think about a time your age helped you bounce vs. break – aren't you amazed at your ability?

Chapter 3. We're Not in Kansas Anymore

> *Do not think of today's failures, but of the success that may come tomorrow. You have set yourselves a difficult task, but you will succeed if you persevere; and you will find a joy in overcoming obstacles.*
>
> Helen Keller

When I was banished from my job in 2008, I did not foresee that the economy's steep nosedive would remind people of the 1930s. Even after three years, we are facing a double-dip recession. A survivor of the economic downturn in 2000, I expected the winds of progress would soon lift us up — like 99% of the rest of the world, I did not sense that a global gale storm was brewing.

One opportunity presented itself shortly after my ouster: I subcontracted with a colleague to write job descriptions for a municipality. Plain vanilla work never tasted so good. Interviews with employees in a variety of roles within a City Hall gave no hint that across America, towns, cities and states would soon be threatened with bankruptcy.

Blissfully unaware of the magnitude of the job climate change, I waited for the clouds to clear. In addition to intermittent consulting work, I paid my share of expenses with unemployment benefits and a modest inheritance from an aunt. Intelligent but uneducated, Aunt Kay walked to work for 40 years, and the day she was forced out, she thought it was an April Fool's joke. Kay never married; she maintained the homestead and willed it to her nieces. A loving, timely gift.

****

For ten months, I made a conscious effort to stay optimistic in the face of diminishing funds and a fuzzy future. I scoured four home-delivered newspapers for upbeat headlines and pasted them on a poster board. Using stamp pads and silver ink, I filled in spaces with huge sunflowers, butterflies and the word "believe." I also tackled a writing project with a girlfriend. Although it was never finished, it kept my creative juices flowing.

Nearly a year later, in 2009, I started a part-time job with a large non-profit agency. I was hired by a woman who had been my consulting partner and who is also a good friend. At the same time, a labor lawyer recommended me for a compensation project; the combination of the part-time job and consulting work boosted my spirits and provided much-needed income.

My new part-time job resembled a management development project I ran early in my career. Funded by a federal stimulus bill, I was charged with hiring six business majors for a one-year program. Participants would gain non-profit experience, and the agency would benefit from their business perspectives. Most non-profit leaders have social service credentials, which typically do not include finance, marketing and operational expertise. The downturn in the economy offered a unique opportunity to bring the two worlds closer together.

Awfully Glad

Some say fall is the true beginning of the business year, and I felt like an eager student as I organized my new program in September 2009. I was so optimistic, a piece I wrote about thankfulness was chosen for a feature in a national newspaper. I outlined giving up my consulting business to accept a job, only to lose it within a year. I expressed appreciation for the new part-time job and my husband's health benefits. And I didn't leave out what really counts:

> *Looking over the past year*
> *I am thankful for*
> *the unemployment checks,*

colleagues who scrounged up work,
and good friends
who are always in my corner...
My employment and retirement future
is fuzzier than last year,
but I was only temporarily
stunned by the ambush...

My boomer brain still functions,
my health is hardy ...
I treasure my little family circle.
My daughter has survived
a series of setbacks,
and my Mom lives alone but says
she doesn't need a thing.

What's not to be thankful for?

A 55+ friend and colleague, who has endured prolonged periods of joblessness, e-mailed and said: "Okay, Pollyanna, be thankful if you want, but I think all this sucks!"

Hiring Youngsters and Oldsters

While my first order of business was to select people
for the stimulus program, I took time to design the
objectives and identify desired candidate
qualifications. Working for someone I trusted and
respected helped bring out the best ideas. We agreed
to strive for diversity — including age, gender,
ethnicity and areas of expertise.

After a rigorous interview and selection process, the
six new hires included three people age 25 or under;
three age 55 or over; three women and three men; and
a mix of racial and religious backgrounds. They
brought skills in the areas of finance, sales and
marketing, operations, quality and safety, and
organizational effectiveness. Two had master's
degrees, one brought military leadership experience,
and all had volunteered in their communities,
including global relief projects. It was thrilling to put
a Dream Team together.

The program was structured to rotate the participants
through three or four assignments within the year.

Identifying relevant projects, structuring the objectives, soliciting performance feedback and documenting results was my responsibility. I also facilitated supervisory training with a professor from a private university and developed an in-house mentoring program.

Savvy, Seasoned Professionals

Doing the actual work was their job, and what a spectacular job they did. Each one of them was a fast learner, highly motivated and flexible. Advanced age did not hinder anyone's performance. To the contrary, the older participants had the benefit of so many work and life experiences, they hit the ground running. They informally coached the early-career group, in exchange for assistance with new technologies, although one 55+ woman was ahead of everyone else when it came to social networking and emerging software.

Within a ten-month period, the team produced lasting products, including workflow recommendations, an enhanced employee newsletter, a framework for maintenance and safety procedures, a speaker's program and reporting protocols. Individuals served on community committees and helped with a variety of events. They had different work styles and strengths, but age didn't matter — we were all there to learn, contribute and, we hoped, have a job waiting for us at the end.

As we approached the end of the program funding, the economy seemed to be getting worse. The non-profit agency that sponsored the program had limited job openings, and most applications submitted through the Internet went unanswered. Or, in one 55+ woman's case, a rapid-fire rejection seemed to lack any human intervention. Things started looking grim, and my efforts to get publicity for the group were ineffective. I was committed to helping them land on their feet, and also had to contemplate my own next move.

Packing Up, Again

When it came to staying solvent, age *did* matter. Two of the "25 and under" group still lived home, so they were not weighted down with heavy fixed expenses. The third was frantically applying for jobs in order to get married and start the American Dream. All were eager to launch their futures and were frustrated.

To different degrees, each of us in the "55+ group" were lugging around a full bag of grown-up bills. With fewer earning years stretching before us, every month without a job would chip away at any chance of enjoying "golden years." Or, more pressing, our ability to hang onto our houses and have health insurance! When one of us was able to comfortably retire early at 62, we all were sincerely happy that someone had made it to the other side.

It started dawning on me that those of us over age 55 were particularly vulnerable in the dreadful job market. I noted that, after performing heroic acrobatic maneuvers to balance careers and families, older women were yesterday's news. Not acting our ages, another 55+ woman and I made a "pinky promise" to help one another land safely.

As part of the pinky promise, Nancy and I brainstormed ways to promote ourselves, including colorful postcards with our photos. There were daily chats to fend off waves of panic, and secrets shared over ice cream cones. We laughed at the absurdity of our situations and swapped stories about adult children, husbands and dogs. We became the kind of friends everyone needs in a crisis.

The stimulus program was disbanded at the end of September 2010. One "25 and under" participant who logged countless hours on job-search engines grabbed a for-profit position and moved out of state, closer to home. The other two people in this age group left without jobs but were employed within six months — but one lacked health benefits.

Surprisingly, the agency found jobs for two women in the 55+ group, but neither was an especially good fit. Both left within four months, one to retire. Nancy landed a good job, using her fund-raising skills from a former life. Fred, another older participant, returned to quality management after a nine-month search and

re-certification classes. I continued to look for jobs
but suspected my best bet was as a consultant.

*The 55+ people I hired into the
stimulus program were stars, just
like the 25-year old group.*

*At 59, I built on 30 years of
experience to quickly design and
manage a jobs program.*

*But our success did not attract
immediate job options.*

Being 55+ did not bode well.

Chapter 4. Left Behind at 55?

We all live in suspense, from day to day, from hour to hour; in other words, we are the hero of our own story.

Mary McCarthy, Writer

Part of my self-promotion was a new web site. I had shut down my first site when I accepted the full-time job in 2008. Fortunately, setting up a web site has become much easier, so I took the DIY approach. A reader and writer at heart, I got the idea to comment on articles from *The New York Times*, *USA Today* and the *Hartford Courant*. My blog replaced my habit of clipping and highlighting articles for my husband and daughter — although sometimes I still can't resist.

On November 2, 2010, my entry was titled "55+ Unite?" Commenting on riots in France over retirement ages, I shared how older people I knew, despite impressive résumés, were receiving rejection letters faster than a speeding bullet. I declared this a Depression, not a Recession, for older workers. And I suggested maybe we should form a collective to put our magnificent selves back to work.

Several people in my professional circle found this entry intriguing — at this point, I was not yet focused on women. But by the end of January 2011, I created a 55+ tab on my web site, and put forth a call to arms:

"55+ Unite" – A Manifesto for Women

Lies, damned lies, and statistics aside, there is compelling evidence that older women are an endangered species in this dreadful job market. By older, we mean first-generation who were liberated from the kitchen and welcomed at grad school.

Women who became role models for running meetings while their kids were throwing up at day care. And we won't go into those awful man-suits with floppy bow ties.

Women aged 55 and over are almost 20% of the female work force, slightly outnumber their male counterparts, and about 40% of them are in management, professional and related occupations. Or, at least they were in 2008, before the market crashed.

They can expect to live another 20+ years, and many need (and want) to keep working — in this way they are equal to men, only their retirement funds are more anemic. Rome was not built in a day, and push come to shove, women were more likely to sacrifice long term career security to keep the home fires burning.

The concept of a glass ceiling is as quaint as a glass slipper for these ladies – they can't even get a foot in the door. In 2006, 25% of employers surveyed

*admitted they were reluctant to hire older workers —
since that sentiment was assuredly under-reported to
begin with, today women over 55 are uninvited on a
grand scale.*

*Fortunately, this pioneer group has unprecedented
education, experience and survivor instincts – not to
mention buying power.   We are a small band of
women who are looking to inspire older working
women to fight back, support one another and
continue to set records in the workplace. While as
individuals we are unemployed or underemployed,
we know we can summon strength from our sisters-
in-arms.*

So, there!

Leaving La-La Land

My networking plan included joining a Board of
Directors for a non-profit that focused on fiscal
literacy and vocational training. From a self-serving
standpoint, it offered me a way to reconnect within
the Hartford community.   In return, I believed I could

offer insights and expertise based on my human resources and consulting experience.

I resigned after six months. Despite the pleasure of working with a talented group of people, I succumbed to a growing sense of cognitive dissonance. Board discussions about helping people open bank accounts and budget their limited dollars struck me as belonging to a simpler time.

If whole countries could not balance their budgets, what did that mean for people with minimal incomes? Or, closer to home, if professionals were losing their jobs, who would help them hang on to their houses? Initially, I told myself to "be the change I wished to see in the world" — that generously sharing my time and talents on behalf of a local charity was a small but meaningful gesture.

Then I realized giving time and talent wasn't enough — I was expected to make rain. I've been on several other non-profit boards, but was not pressured to raise funds. I understood I was expected to donate, which I did. And I attended two development training sessions to get my head around the art of getting others to give. But I wasn't picturing making a pitch to my friends.

At the end of one Board meeting, a member of the development committee introduced an exercise — we were instructed to hand over the names of people in our circle of influence. The purpose was to build a potential donor list. We were assured no one would be contacted without our prior consent.

I grew uneasy, and spoke up. Looking at my target list, the only person in a position to make a donation was my mother, and her mailbox already overflowed with solicitations from religious and civic groups. At 86, she needed to cut back. As for the rest of the people on my list, the picture was bleak: Despite graduate degrees and gobs of professional experience, my closest associates were juggling financial balls of fire.

One was just denied health insurance. Another's house was underwater. Several were unemployed or earning a fraction of previous salaries. I sputtered to

the group that earlier in my career, encouraging co-
workers to consider a donation would have been a no-
brainer. But in my current world, colleagues were
losing sleep over unpaid bills.

The puzzled, concerned looks on the faces around the
table told me they lived in the old-world order. They
had jobs within banking, non-profits and insurance —
industries familiar to me. But based on their follow-
up questions, they did not know professional women
aged 55+ who had been kicked to the curb during the
economic crash. One fellow, who has been a friend for
many years, said, "Georgian, are these women alone?"

Alone, as in no husband with a flush 401K, healthy
pension, small mortgage and affordable health
insurance? That would be "yes." While the other
Board members seemed insulated from the ravages of
the economic crash, I was associated with women who
were struggling for survival. I resolved to spend my
energies addressing issues close to home.

Who Will Help Us Bake the Bread?

Armed with the "55+ Unite Manifesto," a couple of
friends joined me in promoting our issues. At
women's networking sessions, we handed out 5"x7"
cards containing the manifesto and our photos. In
addition to the "55+ Unite" tab on my web site, I
started a group on LinkedIn. We researched statistics
and similar groups, ordered books, visited web sites
and participated in a webinar on The Maturing
Woman. We shared our worries and dreams, and
generated ideas.

Reaction to the manifesto was tepid. There was
generally a sense of "Gee whiz, it sucks to be old."
People would nod and say, "Oh, right," but no one
said, "Let me help." Several people admitted, "Of
course, no one is going to hire an older woman."

I couldn't fault anyone for not knowing where to start
– our dilemma includes global economics,
unemployment, age bias and gender bias. Now that
America has grown all these accomplished working
women, what is she going to do with us? We are too

young for Social Security and too old to be tomorrow's talent. And if the retirement age for Social Security keeps rising, 55 will start to seem young!

No one is swooping in to save us. Despite a surplus of promising ideas, society cannot change fast enough for those of us already 55+. Our best hope is to raise the consciousness of our cohorts, remind ourselves of our brilliance and help at least one other woman to carry on.

Eleanor's husband wisely said, "The only thing we have to fear is fear itself."

We working women age 55+ have to monitor our self-talk and not buy into the statistics about jobs in today's market.

Some hiring managers have a bias in favor of candidates with experience and work maturity. Go find them, and cheer on a friend to do the same.

Chapter 5.   55+ Career Profiles

While our extensive working years cannot be neatly labeled, creating a timeline can help us reflect on major stages in our careers. The following graphic lists the type of work I was doing at different ages, as well when I furthered my education and became a mother. My guess is most men would not mix family and career information, but that is just one of the many ways that we differ!

Author's Career Profile

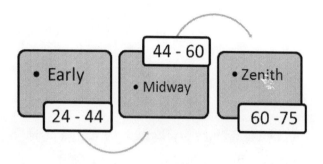

Early: Full-time jobs; advanced degree; motherhood
Midway: Independent consulting; two jobs at 58-60
Zenith: Unemployed! Author & Consultant

During the first twenty years of my career, I worked for three organizations, learned a lot, had seven different jobs and made lasting friendships. Taking the leap into independent consulting was a drastic move, but my career had started to feel stale, my daughter needed to see me more, and the road ahead looked uninviting. Going back to being an employee from 58-60 was unexpected, but worth the ride.

Becoming a published author at 61 was a thrill, and I look forward to the next fifteen years — or more! Following are 55+ Career Profiles of four of my friends. While the timelines are approximate, they create a mosaic that is representative of our age group.

55+ Profile: Pat

Writing pension plans in a barely renovated factory building sounds dreadful, but it was 1976, and dozens of newly hired, recent college graduates created an energetic work environment. The ERISA law had just passed — a complicated piece of legislation — and every pension contract, plan and booklet had to be brought into compliance.

The highly detailed work was not my cup of tea, and for the first time since second grade, I got in trouble for talking. I am still soul mates with Pat, one of my fellow offenders, thirty-five years later. We never lost touch, even though years would fly by without seeing each other.

Filling some free time after my stimulus job ended, I sent her a musical card that blared out Marvin Gaye's song "What's Going On?" I heard from her within days, but learned that her first job after earning a master's of social work had a horrendous caseload, and she left after five years. Her brave story of early retirement followed by acing her education in a new field held such promise. She was on the job hunt, but the economy was not cooperating.

With both of us between jobs, we had time to travel the 50 miles between our homes, and held late-night cell phone sessions. We attended women's networking events and wore sparkly headbands given out as party-favors. At 60, you can dare to look silly.

Pat generously brought her social work skills to the "55+ Unite" quest, including giving me a copy of the ground-breaking book, *The First Sex*. I vicariously celebrated the birth of her first grandchild, and she helped me stay out of the way at my daughter's horse show.

Job opportunities were scarce, and Pat was getting discouraged. When Pat was afraid she was washed up before really getting started, a trusted woman in her field said: "Don't think that way – you have a lot to contribute." Together they brainstormed ways for her to complete outstanding educational requirements, and she recently accepted a job that will help her advance in her field. I won't get to see her as much, but we are closer than ever.

Pat's Career Profile

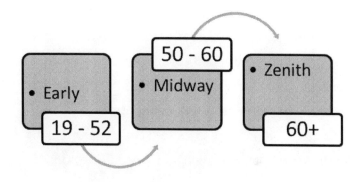

Early: Full-time jobs; motherhood
Midway: BS/MSW; Field work
Zenith: Unemployed! Didn't give up; new job.

In a more-perfect world, Pat would be earning twice her new salary. But today's job market realities for a woman 55+ presented a dilemma – keep competing with younger applicants for precious few jobs, or take the lower-paying job and get on with it? When giving HR advice, I usually caution against being underemployed. Overqualified employees often get themselves in trouble by raising issues and stating opinions.

But in Pat's case, the fact that the new job provides the opportunity to complete her clinical requirements for an L.C.S.W. designation was cause for careful consideration. From a financial standpoint, she can count on early retirement earnings and health benefits. The cherry on top was that Pat was familiar with the management group, from previous legislative activities. The job is also located close to her daughter and new grandchild, which adds a work-life bonus.

To me, Pat is a role model for women who go back to school and start second careers. But things don't always work out smoothly. One significant part of Pat's story is the influence her trusted advisor had on her when she thought of giving up. Because her advisor was in her same field, she had the credibility to pull Pat out of a spiral of negative thinking. A powerful example of one 55+ woman helping another.

55+ Profile: Thelma

We were a winning team in our company's fat-club:
Between us, we lost 75 pounds in seven months.
Sitting near each other, Thelma and I formed a
partnership that kept us on track between weekly
weigh-ins. It's pretty hard to justify a slice of that
birthday cake in the conference room when you have
to walk by Jiminy Cricket's workstation. We were
determined, but kept a sense of humor.

Thelma's data management job was cut in a round of
downsizing, and her next move was most uncertain.
Like many women, she had spent the first part of her
life working part-time while raising children. Her
intelligence, work ethic and detail orientation opened
doors for her when she wanted to work full-time.
When I met Thelma, she had over fifteen years of
experience with banks and health care companies.

At 55+, she still needed to work, but was tempted to
shift gears and work in an area she was passionate
about, such as a library, or with dogs. Her husband's

job provided health benefits, so she had some flexibility. On a personal level, her dad became very ill soon after Thelma was laid off, and she was grateful for the time they could spend together.

About a year after losing her job, a unique opportunity presented itself. Thelma's niece just had twins, and the new mom had a high-powered job. Would Thelma be interested in being a nanny?

At 55+, Thelma is now caring for two active toddlers, and although her job offers less certainty than what she is used to, she is going with the flow. Her experience as a stay-at-home mom is serving her well, and she is feeling more alive than when she sat behind a computer all day.

Thelma is someone I would characterize as wise – she is resilient, makes good judgments, puts things in perspective and laughs at herself. She generously shares whatever she knows, and is curious about things she has yet to learn. I think those two girls are very lucky to have her guidance.

Thelma's Career Profile

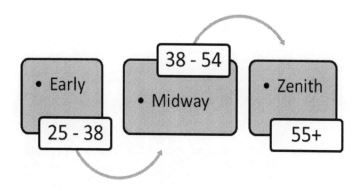

Early: Part-time jobs; motherhood
Midway: Full-time jobs; hobbies
Zenith: Unemployed! Nanny

Thelma's decision to drop out of corporate life was primarily fueled by the lack of job opportunities. Earning a mid-range salary in exchange for being a dependable, accurate worker is not an easy proposition for a woman 55+, in the current economy.

Our workforce lost a solid performer, to the benefit of an ambitious mother with twins. As children grow quickly, Thelma may have to choose whether to pursue a similar job outside the family or try to return to the business arena. Health benefits could become an issue if her husband's job conditions change.

Thelma's situation meets her current needs, and she is confident enough to handle things as circumstances dictate. She comes from a large family, and being able to take care of her brother's grandchildren is a special privilege for her.

I particularly admire Thelma's ability to take on a whole new role without looking back. Having a realistic view of her job predicament and being open to new vistas, she displays the emotional maturity and humility that allow her to bend, not break.

55+ Profile: Gayle

I met Gayle when she ran an independent bookstore with her husband. It was a magical place, a spa for my brain. After hours of writing job descriptions for engineers, I would stop by her store before picking my daughter up from school. Located in the center of a downtown decorated with Victorian streetlights, it was an oasis from my nose-to-the-grindstone pace.

When they closed the store, my trips to town were flatter. Post Office, bank, dentist. Although Gayle lived near me, our connection was within the walls of that little shop around the corner. But our houses are within a five-minute drive, so I started picking her up to head for a breakfast nook that is straight out of Mayberry RFD.

But our lives were not following a cheery script. We both had enjoyed successful careers, but were stalled at 55+. I was laid off, and her shop closing was linked with the poor economy. What could we do to turn things around?

Armed with a master's in liberal studies and early writing success, Gayle encouraged me in my quest to become a more established author. While she shared some of those same goals, she also needed to find a way to earn money, now.

Gayle parlayed her education, language skills and bookstore experience into a part-time editorial position for a monthly magazine. She successfully competed against hundreds of other applicants in a process she likened to Dancing with the Stars. A challenging job at any age, I suspect her mid-life brain comes through with razor-sharp decisions and solutions in the deadline-driven world of publishing.

Planning to work another fifteen years, Gayle constantly brainstorms ways to get more momentum in her career. Former luxuries, like travel and seminars, are on the back burner, for now.

Gayle's Career Profile

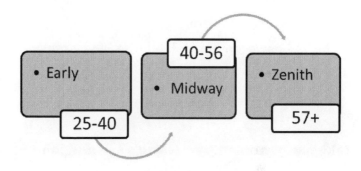

Early: Part-time jobs; advanced degree; motherhood
Midway: Full-time job; retail owner
Zenith: Unemployed! Magazine editor

While Gayle's editorial job has a lot of responsibility, it is only part-time. Although she picks up occasional consulting assignments, including editing two of my e-books, she wants to increase her income. Ideally, she needs a job with health benefits. In a better economy, a person with management expertise and a graduate degree from a prestigious university would not have a problem filling her dance card. Even if that person was 55+.

Another dilemma for Gayle is finding outlets for her many artistic talents – frustrated artists are almost a cliché, but having to worry about meeting monthly bills prevents her from fully expressing her creativity.

Like many women 55+, Gayle's age and job situation contributed to a perfect storm when the economy nosedived. Gracefully accepting getting older is a lot harder when it seems to be held against you. Living with financial uncertainty does demand that we become the heroines of our own story, and having a supportive friend helps.

55+ Profile: Jo-Ann

The friend who hired me to run the stimulus program also nagged me to write. We are both Capricorns, and we try to break that stodgy mold by exchanging creative birthday gifts. She gave me a T-shirt that warned: "Be Careful, or You Will End Up in My Novel."

I hung up the Writing Muse she gave me on the lampshade by my bed – a place where I often write. A paper angel with butterfly wings, she proclaims "I Love to Write." On her full skirt is a quote from James Michener: "I love the swirl and swing of words as they tangle with human emotions." Another gift was an old-world, exquisitely bound notebook. Jo-Ann inscribed: "Georgian, if you write a story about me, change the facts to protect the innocent. P.S. I want Diane Keaton to play me in the movie."

For ten years, she constantly encouraged me to make more use of my writing talents. When she was invited to write an article for a human resources magazine, she included me. Mine was published, not hers, but Jo-Ann was happy for me. Not surprisingly, she is the one who alerted me to the "call for authors" that led to my first e-book.

Jo-Ann started working right out of high school, ran a horse facility while holding down responsible full-time jobs and earned a B.S. and M.B.A. in her 30s. She gained extensive management experience working for public companies before branching off to independent consulting. For five years, we partnered on consulting projects, and when she took a full-time job, I wished her well. That turned full circle when she hired me five years later to run the stimulus jobs program.

Her latest job ended after she built a first-class human resources department -- mission accomplished, time to move on. At 62, she is contemplating next steps. A shrewd businesswoman, she can probably afford to retire, but then what? Walking away from the job market at this age is likely a permanent decision. Jo-Ann has worked for over 40 years – will she be content to be "on vacation" for maybe the next twenty years?

Jo-Ann's Career Profile

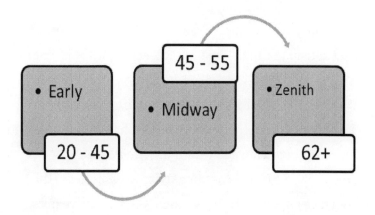

Early: Full-time jobs; MBA; business owner
Midway: Consultant; business owner; HR executive
Zenith: Unemployed! Retire?

Jo-Ann's dilemma is not strictly financial. She likely
can retire, but then what? A driver-driver for forty
years, how she would plan to spend the next twenty
years is a question men traditionally face.

Helen Hayes said, "If you rest, you rust." So should Jo-Ann struggle to find another job in this economy, out of fear that there is a narrow window of opportunity? Or perhaps consider becoming a mentor to women at an earlier stage in their careers? Would that satisfy her high need for achievement?

While Jo-Ann's problem is preferable to that of Pat, Thelma or Gayle, the scarcity of jobs leaves her with fewer options than she would have in a healthy economy. Settling is not her style, so essentially, the shortage of good jobs for women 55+ may drive her decision.

On the surface, Jo-Ann does not seem disadvantaged by ageism and sexism in this poor economy. But if she makes a significant life decision based on a sense of diminished opportunities, she is negatively affected. As in Thelma's case, the American workforce may lose another valuable contributor.

Your Own Career Profile

Now it's your turn to create a graphic picture of your career. What ages would you consider as your early career? Is there a point at which you transitioned into another field, or changed your job circumstances?

When did family or educational milestones occur? Remember the example of Pat, who completed her undergraduate and graduate degrees in her 50s, after taking an early retirement.

If your 55+ box has unknowns, try completing it with different endings! Think big, and have fun envisioning yourself wearing different hats.

Your Own Career Profile

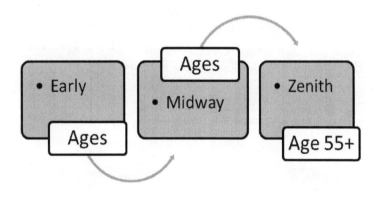

Early: Jobs; education; family

Midway: Jobs; transitions

Zenith: Current situation; next steps

As you reflect about how you got to where you are, jot down accomplishments, enjoyable jobs and people who were helpful in your career advancement. When you reach Chapter 8, "Looking Back to Move Forward," these notes will help you create next steps.

What is your career profile telling you? Write the final chapter to your own story – how would you like to describe your work life at 55+? Think positive, and tell your capable, sub-conscious mind to start figuring out how to make it happen.

Chapter 6. If Not Now, When?

> *Everyone has talent. What is rare is the courage to follow the talent to the dark place where it leads.*
>
> Erica Jong
> Writer

In a steady state, it is easy to push talent aside — other commitments provide convenient excuses for not developing natural gifts, especially as we age. As Charles Schultz, the wise creator of the comic strip "Peanuts," said, "Life is like a ten-speed bicycle. Most of us have gears we never use."

But when pressed beyond comfort, those talents can burst forth. They did for me. In the following sections I share my story of being a late-blooming writer — around 55, it seemed like a hidden source was pushing me toward a dream I had stuffed away. I was taking small steps, without anticipating that I would one day look down and see I climbed a mountain.

Kicking Out the Inner Critic

I flirted with the idea of being a writer in college, but it seemed lofty. Despite encouragement from a professor my freshman year, I veered off to become an English teacher – not that there were any jobs when I graduated in 1973. Well, one principal offered me a job that disappeared over the summer, and another said it was really too bad I couldn't coach the cheerleaders.

Having a way with words helped me ace history finals and stay in touch with my grandparents in Kansas. In the corporate world, communication skills are critical, and although one boss told me I needed to write more succinctly, my way with words was an asset.

As a harried working mother, I produced the newsletter for my daughter's parochial grade school for several years. Initially with a partner, and then as a solo act, I stalked teachers for stories and thanked donors for giving. I profiled successful graduates, who fondly recalled their early days with the three R's and the holy trinity.

Breaking Loose at 55

In 2005, I received an award for an article I wrote about my daughter's horse passion. The piece appeared on the back page of a dressage magazine, and described her decision to home school at 16 to jump-start her equestrian career. One judge praised my work for what it didn't say, as well as what was revealed.

Little did the critic know that one piece I left out was a near-death accident earlier that year. While leading a horse into the barn for the night, Alexis was kicked in the face by the horse and found convulsing in a pool of blood. Life Star was grounded, so she flew down the highway in a blaring ambulance. I had turned 55 just three days before.

Miraculously, her brain was intact, and an eye specialist said she came within a hair's breadth of being blinded. My husband and I got to her side a half-hour after she was admitted to the trauma unit. She was conscious and made eye contact with me, offering a tight smile. My husband noted that her forehead injury was shaped like a horseshoe.

At the time I wrote the article, Alexis had returned to her barn job after a three-month recovery. Her devoted plastic surgeon advised her to wear protective goggles over the three plates in her forehead, which proved impractical. The finger that was crushed as she defended her face was also fortified with a plate, and she discovered that braiding manes was excellent hand therapy.

My words in the article reflected the passion that pulled Alexis through a tremendous trial. I told her story in a lighthearted way, but her single-mindedness was evident. I wrote the article with the greatest of ease – my inner critic was sent to sit in the corner.

The accident that smashed my daughter's face and hand also broke open my soul. My egg was cracked by the early news that she had been trampled by a horse and taken to a hospital – status unknown. Wondering if she was still alive, the gray winter air around me seemed to vaporize into embers. My life paused, and the world turned eerily silent and still.

A few months into her recovery, I wrote a five-page account of the accident and its aftermath. I felt compelled to capture the intensity of the experience, to acknowledge the many acts of compassion, and to document her brave spirit. Since my mother's large family is dispersed across the Midwest, I wanted them to know what happened. Otherwise, they would only hear that she was kicked by a horse and is now fine.

I wrote freely and with purpose. While I took time to polish the words and structure the sections, I didn't worry about being judged. This was my story, as a mother. Alexis knew I wrote it, but never read it. Neither did my husband – they both lived it.

That heartfelt piece, intended only for family and friends, helped me break through my self-doubt. Reaction to my style of writing, as well as the dramatic content, was very positive. I left a copy with my dad's doctor, who called me to say, "I really enjoyed reading this – and not just because you are George's daughter, or because of the terrible accident – I write for medical journals, and this is excellent."

Around this time I attended several annual writers' conferences hosted by *The Hartford Courant*. Squeezed between young reporters in large conference rooms, I soaked in how authors described their writing lives and techniques. I also studied writing by reading books such as Stephen King's excellent guide, *On Writing*.

New Feats at 55+

I started speaking of myself as a writer, and soon landed an opportunity to produce a series of articles for a construction magazine. I had taught over 1,000 plumbing contractors in a business class for continuing education credit, and used those experiences to think up topics with general appeal.

A chance meeting with a magazine publisher led to writing assignments for a painting and decorating association. As I did with the parochial school graduates, I interviewed contractors and manufacturers to promote products and events. Giving up those writing gigs was one thing I regretted about accepting a full-time job at 58.

Rejoining the corporate world was exhausting – and not because of my age. I stepped into a very broad job with very few resources, and was part of an effort to take the organization to a new level. But I still wanted to find time to write. Shortly before I was summarily dismissed in 2008, I signed up for a few hypnosis sessions. My goal was to write a book. I wondered if my inner critic had settled back into my brain, or if I was just too tired to write. Soon I had time to find out.

Once I lost my job, I started to collaborate with a good friend and colleague who also was between jobs. Our plan was to combine our writing and artistic talents to produce cartoons that dispensed words of wisdom to working women. We got stuck at several points, and before we could push through, she moved across the country. Our friendship thrived, but the idea went dormant.

One day in 2010, I got an email while working part-time at the non-profit agency. The woman I was working for wrote: "FYI – A Call for Authors – This is right up your alley." It was an invitation to consider writing an e-book about business. The organization guides you through the process, and your book joins an e-library that is made available through an online subscription.

Intrigued, I responded to the email, but when I did not hear back I dismissed it as one more far-flung Internet offering. But when I found myself at home again, looking for work after the non-profit program ended, I chanced upon that same organization. I came up empty the first time, but what's to lose?

This time I referenced my new web site/blog, as well as the on-line contractor articles. Within days, a polite woman with a warm voice called me and said she thought my contractor articles were interesting, despite the plumbing backdrop. Would I be open to scheduling an online meeting to explore working together?

You bet. Within two weeks, I signed an agreement to write an e-book on cross-training. No money up front, but commission on whatever sells. Oh, and ten complimentary copies! Since I could write the book in between looking for work, it seemed like a great place to start – if not now, when?

Almost Effortless

The publisher's structured approach helped me focus on my chosen topic within a prescribed number of pages. Having to follow a format, including quick quizzes and case studies, kept me focused on tasks, vs. doubts. I owed a first draft within ninety days, so my mission was clear.

My husband was super-supportive. He carefully read each section and told me when something didn't make sense or needed more explanation. I delivered my draft weeks ahead of time, and my publishing editor suggested I add some sections, which I completed within a month. So why did I wait until I was 61 to do something that was relatively easy?

First off, it wouldn't have been so easy without so much experience. My writing was based on a career of over thirty years. I ran a management development and mentoring program in 1980 and created an experimental office of self-managed teams in 1987. My consulting work with over fifty companies in a dozen industries helped me compare and contrast different ways of developing talent. All of that experience was within the context of a master's of organizational behavior that I earned thirty-five years ago.

Second, I'd been writing for public audiences for five years and had come to view myself as a legitimate author. Previously, writing was more of a gift that I used in my personal life; I kept diaries and wrote tributes about family members. Now I believed I earned membership in the author's club.

Third, getting older forced me to do it, now. While I feel my intellectual powers are in fine shape, the reality is that my future productive years are preciously fewer. Actually, having a short time horizon has a silver lining. The burden of leaving options open for future years is lifted, and it is easier to focus on the here and now.

In my 20s, becoming an author seemed impractical. In my 40s, I used my writing skills as a consultant.

At 55, I sent my inner critic packing.

Getting older is not the end of dreams. What talents, skills or dreams might you weave into your final career chapter?

Chapter 7. Friends & Companions

> *I always felt that the great high privilege, relief and comfort of friendship was that one had to explain nothing.*
>
> Katherine Mansfield
> Writer

One is Silver, the Other Gold ...

We sang about the value of keeping friends as Brownies, and Betty White urges us not to "let friends fly away." I regret that I have let some friendships fade away, and chide myself for sometimes being distracted when someone needed me. But I am very lucky to be surrounded by a strong web of women.

From High School to Hollywood

It was 1965, and the Beatles wanted to hold our hands.
Despite getting a scholarship to an all-girls Catholic
high school, I convinced my parents to let me leave
after my freshman year. Looking back, it was a great
learning environment, but I was boy-crazy.

An intense Italian girl with darting, dark eyes sat next
to me in a homeroom in our blue-collar high school.
It was my luck that our last names were close in the
alphabet. New to the public school system, I was an
unknown, an outsider. Abby was part of a clique from
junior high, but followed no one's rules.

Our friendship carried us through boring English
classes and a serious car crash. She became a teen
mom, which she later chronicled in a book about her
misspent youth. But first, she graduated from
Wesleyan and Columbia.

Even though I was 40 when the book was published, I
was hesitant to have my parents read my cameo
appearance in her story. Not to worry. My mom was

thrilled for her, but was always too busy to sit down and read. My dad read the book cover to cover, and said, "You were really a good friend to her."

Well, the book went Hollywood, and my mom and I were invited to the New York premiere. 9/11 demolished those plans, but I saw the movie eight times, with different people. Thankfully, my character was combined with others and I soaked in the excitement without being a focus of local gossip. Not that I've ever cared that much about conventional rules, either.

Abby's now working on a memoir about her spiritual quest, and sent me some draft pages. Reading them on my living room couch, I debated about offering my opinion – after all, she is a full-time author and professor. I took the chance of sharing my thoughts, which generated a rich give-and-take. Along with a woman who has a degree in religious studies, I accepted her invitation to be a reader of her proposal pages.

By offering to help, I got a peek into the mind of her publisher, and flexed my own editing muscles. Abby's sizable advance came through just before Christmas of 2010, and she treated me at a restaurant of my choice to celebrate. Forty-five years of friendship is dove-tailing into a writer's dream.

Everlasting Career Chums

Postcard from Banff National Park, Canada's Rockies -- Dear Georgian: The camping part has its rough moments but the hikes are extraordinary. Unparalleled turquoise lakes, views of mountains and glaciers, the great feeling of being happily exhausted after an 11 mile hike. Always have a hard time getting into the swing of the group stuff, but holding my own. Tent is surrounded by mountains – oh so ever changing in the sunlight, clouds or rain. Tomorrow going to a 9000' peak, with a 2,800 elevation gain in the hill. The view should be spectacular. Love, Liz. (Age 59: August, 2011)

When I first met Liz, Helen and Margaret in 1978, we took ourselves very seriously. Our mission was to uphold personnel policies and ensure competitive pay for 40,000 employees in a Hartford-based insurance company. Closing in on 30, we wore business suits and sensible pumps. No bright nail polish or dangly earrings to distract us from our purpose.

Not that we were goody two-shoes. I prominently displayed books about how to succeed in a man's world, and nominated guys for the Piggy's Club, as penalties for chauvinistic shenanigans. And while I was working on a wardrobe that befitted my next promotion, I didn't always wear a bra.

Rumor had it we were known as Helen's Henchwomen — I guess we threatened to take all the fun out of company politics. Our seriousness did pay off — we've enjoyed a lot of success, and have shared some great stories.

Helen and Margaret finished their careers in the global insurance world, including an executive post and being stationed in Hong Kong. Liz embarked on a gutsy change that was 360 degrees away from job descriptions and pay surveys: She went back to college for a degree in landscape architecture and opened her own business. She then circled back to her hometown on the Cape and started hosting girls-only getaways.

We've analyzed, pondered, celebrated and lamented the mysteries of man, woman, birth, death and infinity. Raising teenagers and almost losing a teenager. Jobs, unemployment and retirement. Travel, hiking and gardening. Books, movies and facts stranger than fiction. Losing moms and dads. Miscarriages. Sons and daughters. Holidays, horrible days, and cancer.

Friends for thirty-five years, these three women have listened attentively to my attempts at writing, always responding with: "This is good stuff – keep it up." I hope I have been equally supportive. Even when plagued with self-doubt, we believe in each other.

Ladies' getaway at the Cape. The tides
turned during our nature walk, but we
were undaunted. I was closing in on 55.

Rose, My Fairy Godmother

A Disneyland hotel lobby was an unlikely place to get my daughter's IQ tested, but my Mom's 55-year-old cousin sized up five-year-old Alexis within a flash. "She is bright, bright, bright – and the teachers are not going to like her." Okay, that's good, I guess?

Rose is the friendliest, most down-to-earth Ph.D. I ever met, but when using her expertise, she doesn't mince words. Then again, she probably spared me the pain of describing what it would mean to shepherd my only child through the mainstream. I'd find out soon enough, on my own.

As we left the lobby and were approaching a busy boulevard to get to our cars, Alexis held out both arms and instructed us to stand back. Being a clueless mom, I got impatient with her outburst. Really! We were four adults, and she was five years old. In the kindest voice, Rose said, "You know why she is doing that, right?" Not giving me time to embarrass myself, she continued, "It's because she is so smart." Oh, right.

Well, Rose *was* right. Her informal IQ assessment amazingly matched the score given to Alexis at the end of first grade — she was tested because she wasn't reading. All year, I had dutifully performed the flash card drill, but Alexis didn't suffer fools gladly, and tossed the cards in the air. Rose, help!

Rose didn't hesitate. In a snail-mail era, she guided me over the phone from California to Connecticut, and mailed a tailored reading plan that a local tutor agreed to implement. She based the plan on the battery of tests conducted by a school psychologist, and praised his report. Tactfully, Rose reminded me that part of my daughter's difficulties stemmed from the fact she knew her teacher didn't like her!

Her plan worked. Over the summer, Alexis was tutored four hours a day, five days a week, and gained six months of reading progress between first and second grade. As a graduate-level educator, Rose clearly understood the system. In no uncertain terms, she told me to pull out all the stops. The grade school train was pulling out of the station, and if my daughter wasn't on it, she would be left behind. It was that simple.

Rose has celebrated my daughter's progress for twenty years, and I was thrilled that they joined up when Alexis went to California for her twenty-first birthday. Rose's cheerleading extends to me, as well.

After reviewing some of the impassioned letters I sent to grade school teachers (who ended up not liking me much, either), Rose encouraged my writing efforts. She's a trusted reader of material I wouldn't show anyone else.

Rose is restricted from traveling long distances for health reasons, and we missed each other several times when I was on the West Coast for business. Despite our closeness, I haven't seen her in person for these twenty years. She has been a constant source of encouragement — kind of like a fairy godmother. I really should get on a plane and go see her, right?

Pure Spirits

> *Everyone knows how wonderful it is to have a dog. That's what makes them a (kidnapping) target.*
>
> Lisa Peterson, AKC spokeswoman
> Article by Laura Petrecca - *USA Today* 8/23/11

All you owners of Yorkies, Pomeranians and other small dogs can rest assured that my husband will not pay an abductor to steal your best friend. While the bad economy is causing a spike in dog-snatching, the man in my house is largely immune to the charms of a panting pooch.

With the exception of a regal springer spaniel who lived with us many years ago, my husband has a history of mutual mistrust with dogs. Back in the day, he delivered milk and newspapers, making him fair game for freely roaming canines. Even Hans, my family's gentle German shepherd, tried to bite him when he transformed from my brother's best buddy into my serious boyfriend.

I, on the other hand, cherish four-legged friends; a frustrated rancher, my dad kept horses, dogs and cats on our property, as well as a few chickens. But I don't steal dogs, I rescue them. Or rather, I let them rescue me.

****

In 2006, when my daughter, Alexis, moved back home after a careless misdiagnosis trashed her health, she sought the solace of a dog. The sadness of her situation must have registered with my husband, as he silently stood by during the quest for a canine companion. Soon a dog would be moving in, too!

Alexis' Internet search zeroed in on Portuguese pointers, a rare and ancient breed. I took it as a celestial sign that one of the few breeders in the country was within spitting distance. And so began our adventures with our Perfectly Precious Portuguese Pointer Puppies, aka Thing 1 and Thing 2.

Technically, Kona was not a puppy when Alexis coaxed her into the house. The color of light coffee, she was about a year old and suffered a social disorder. The breeder had health problems of her own, and Kona missed out on some essential training. Alexis wanted a one-woman dog, and Kona was overqualified. Sold.

Like Mary's Little Lamb, Kona waited in the car during college classes, slept in Alexis' room and was in a crate when her person was gone. She was terrified of me, so we devised a system with a long leash. When it was my turn to put her on the backyard run, I grabbed or stepped on the leash, avoiding close contact. Texting came in handy if my daughter left the house and forgot to attach the lifeline: "Leash!"

At 57, chasing after a dog that acted like I was swinging a hatchet was not always amusing. Nor were the scratches in the windowsill, the torn rug from a flipped cage, or the loud, frantic barking. Losing my patience over such inconsequential things was humbling. As Alexis nailed it, "Fate puked me back on our front porch," and I was complaining about the most positive thing in her life.

Five years later, Kona is worth her forty-five pounds in gold. She is highly sensitive, kind, and would take a bullet for Alexis. In the dark days when fair-weather friends forgot to call, Kona was steadfast.

About a year after Kona joined our clan, our riches doubled. Working with the breeder, Alexis was starting to leash-train a puppy when it flipped over in excitement, and HOWLED. A $300 vet bill ruled out a hip injury, but recommended swimming therapy. We have an ample back yard.

"Fancy That" wouldn't go in the plastic pool, but Kona enthusiastically splashed around — it helped her decide that we were friendly folks, after all. By the time Fancy healed herself, winter was approaching. Hearing she would spend it in an outdoor kennel, I declared that we needed to keep her. Soon I was calling the dogs "Thing 1 and Thing 2" — like the Dr. Seuss characters, they turned the house upside down. More often, my husband called them the "goddamn dogs."

Fancy, a polar opposite to Kona, galloped through the house, chewing cell phones, glasses, remote controls, shoes and lingerie — earning the alias of "Fancy Pants." She is exuberant and will not be insulted. I once swatted at her with a broom, and she looked at me quizzically: Kona was watching, and never forgot.

I now think the dogs created a healthy distraction during a time when our little family seemed under siege. It was therapeutic to complain about them, because they presented fairly simple problems. More importantly, they loved living with us and thought we were pretty perfect, too.

As Alexis regrouped, her Doctor Doolittle tendencies blossomed. She expanded her interests to fish tanks, and then bought a small parrot, a green conure, that perched on her shoulder and shared pancakes with peanut butter. Of course, he needed company, so was joined by a few parakeets. Our new feathered friends mostly lived in a space above the garage that formerly housed plumbing supplies. Once Alexis became more active, the birds flew the coop; she reluctantly gave them to another animal lover.

The latest spirit in our morality play sneaked in on little cat paws. Pokey was rescued from an abandoned barn, and was two-plus pounds of fluff. The idea was to keep him at the farm where Alexis boarded a horse, but all was not well with Pokey.

Or me, either. At 59, I had lost my senior human resources job, was collecting unemployment, helping a dying aunt who had no children and looking for my next job. Not exactly the perfect conditions to welcome another lost soul — but who can resist a tiny cat with six toes, a white bib and serious medical issues?

Two years later, Pokey has gained ten pounds, despite suffering seizures and having significant plumbing problems. Daily, we shoot four medications down his little kitty gullet. Consequently, he is relatively healthy, but vulnerable. Thanks to our vet, some feline specialists have consulted free of charge, as our cat is such a rare case.

Rare, or magical? My husband has fallen in love with Pokey, and that sentiment has rippled into a greater appreciation of Thing 1 and Thing 2. Alexis and I are astounded.

Spending money on animals while unemployed, and caring for them while our lives are stalled, seems illogical. As we age, we may resist the chaos that comes with keeping pets. I vote for opening your heart to a dog, a cat, or even a bird. I believe our animal friends are pure spirits that keep us from becoming brittle.

Fancy & Kona, under the kitchen table

**Pokey perched on top of the
kitchen table. Never say never.**

Having even one person who cares about the particulars of your situation makes it more bearable.

With all the progress since the '60s, working women still find themselves in DIY mode.

Friends can't redesign the world, but they can open a release valve – even if they have to use paws!

Chapter 8. Looking Back to Blast Forward

One timeless technique that I learned while building
self-managed teams is called a pigtail. It is a model for
looping back to reflect on, and learn from,
organizational events. As a facilitator, I would stand in
front of a group that just completed a task or project.
Drawing four columns on a flip chart, I would fill in
responses to the following questions:

~ What just happened?

~ Why did it happen – what caused us to do it?

~ What can we learn from it?

~ What are implications for next steps? Or — so what,
   therefore?

You may recognize this curlicue exercise as a shortcut
for double-loop learning. Peter Senge's classic book
The Fifth Discipline defines learning organizations. If

you aren't familiar with the book, it makes a good case for being more thoughtful, systematic and generous at work.

The "pigtail" can be used to reflect on our own lives. Arriving at 55+, we have a lot of material to work with! In fact, we run the risk of being flooded by so many events that it is hard to unravel cause and effect. But taking stock at 55+ is an essential part of staying in the game. I suggest starting by thinking about your 25-year-old self, because by then, most of us were launching our adult lives. Then, revisit your 40-year-old self to check for patterns and emerging strengths.

The following story describes a defining moment in my life, at age 25. What I learned about myself through a tragic family situation surprised me, and stayed true. In fact, those lessons are still relevant for me today, at 61. While thankfully all our stories are not so intense, a crisis does bring out our core capacities, and helps us grow. As Eleanor Roosevelt said, "Women are like teabags. We don't know our true strength until we are in hot water."

Using my story as an example, you are then invited to reflect on the strengths that have gotten you this far. While it is never too late to learn, being keenly aware of your own traits and talents helps you make savvy career decisions.

Surviving & Thriving

Flying was in my blood, but it scared me. My great-grandmother, Zerilda, flew from California to visit us in Connecticut in 1960, and I remember being so impressed with her bravery. She was about 75, and clearly accustomed to adventure. I guess growing up in a sod house in North Dakota fortified her for whatever life flung her way.

The next year, my maiden flight was with my family to visit relatives in Kansas, and my older brother, Michael, teased me that we were going to crash. That seemed like a distinct possibility, and while I probably bragged to my friends that I flew TWA, I was glad to get home, safe and sound.

My dad was a crew chief in WWII, and saw a lot of action from the window of a PBY. My mom worked for 30+ years at an aircraft company, and I met Santa at Christmas parties in the plant. Michael started flying while attending a community college in Traverse City, Michigan, and decided to become a professional pilot. For starters, he logged as much air time as he could afford.

One night I said to my mom, "You know, what Michael does is very dangerous." I can't say I had a premonition, but whenever I flew with him, I felt uneasy. Then again, I also was afraid of the horse he rode bareback, so that was typical me.

Michael was drafted for the Vietnam War, and like our dad, he trained as a crew chief. He could have signed on as a pilot, but wanted to minimize his time in the military. He ended up being an air traffic controller for helicopters at an Army base, one step away from direct combat.

After discharge, he attended flight school in Ardmore, Oklahoma, courtesy of the GI Bill. He was then recruited as the manager and chief pilot at a fledgling airport just outside of Charlotte, in a town named Indian Trail. He also taught a course in instrument flying at a local college.

Michael was in his glory, and I was happy for him. Only siblings, we were especially close. When I married his best friend, also a pilot and a war veteran, it strengthened our ties – although I'm not sure my brother predicted a long and happy union. Having lived with us both, he shook his head and said, "East meets West."

My husband and I flew with Michael to go skiing in Vermont, across the patchwork farm land of the Midwest, and even over my office building in Hartford, at night. Looking down from a small plane is magical, and I learned to fight off my fear by studying the small-scale scenery.

Michael followed his passion, but it *was* dangerous. When he was 28, and I was 25, his plane crashed in Wilmington, North Carolina. He was piloting a charter flight for a group of wrestlers, headed to a posh resort area. They survived, although I doubt any of them resumed their careers. Michael also survived, but was totally disabled by a traumatic brain injury.

His accident, and the experience of helping to watch out for him over the remaining thirteen years of his life, changed my world view. I became a fearless advocate on his behalf, challenging doctors and fighting for VA benefits. The medical knowledge I gained in my first job as a disability examiner helped me read medical reports and ask informed questions. My inner warrior roared.

My mother was the true hero in this story, but I played a strong supporting role. I'm not sure Michael approved, but I sang to him – even though my husband nudges me if I sing in church. One favorite was "Michael, Row the Boat Ashore" — I really belted out the part that goes … "Sister, help to trim the sails."

In hindsight, I am astonished that despite this tragedy, I worked, finished grad school and stayed married. My daughter was born six months before Michael died: I was 38, he was 41. Ironically, I overcame my fear of flying, and good thing, as I later traveled a lot for business – sometimes in small planes.

But I was struck by something a psychologist told me soon after the accident. I was worried I was going crazy, mostly because I was in such pain. I explained how my high school sweetheart was killed in Vietnam when I was 19, leaving a diamond ring on deposit at Michael's Jewelers. And that his next younger brother was killed nine months later, on Mother's Day, in a freak twist of fate.

In my logical way, I wondered why I felt like I was coming unglued. "I thought I already learned that life is not fair – that you lose people you love – why am I having such a hard time with this?" He responded that in some ways, each loss gets harder, because we know what we are in for.

This notion was captured in a classic comic strip of "For Better or Worse" by Lynn Johnston. As a young boy, the son, Michael, is refusing to get out of the car to say goodbye to his grandparents, after an enjoyable summer visit. When his grandmother points out that Elizabeth, his younger sister, "doesn't mind goodbyes" he wails, "That's because she doesn't know how <u>LONG</u> they are!"

In dealing with my brother's imprisonment within his own body, I discovered that keeping open to the pain was the only way to bend, not break. I forged a new relationship with Michael, even though he was trapped between heaven and earth. His devastating disabilities added another dimension to my life; as his little sister, I was brave and bold.

Michael -- doing what he loved. 1975

Time changes our perspectives, but at 61, here are some positive things I learned about myself through Michael's accident and our thirteen-year journey:

1. I have a <u>bias for action</u>. As Michael's situation got bleaker, my husband would say, "Well, what can you do?" I'd reply, "I don't know, but I am going to do something."

2. <u>I could forgive nine people for letting me down, if just one person extended a hand</u>. Sometimes, even a stranger can make all the difference.

3. I learned to <u>challenge experts</u>. Michaels' first doctor admitted neurology was in the stone ages, but those who followed acted certain, even when they didn't have answers.

4. When things got overwhelming, I found I could <u>reframe the situation and set small, short-term goals.</u> I got better at warding off catastrophic thinking.

5. <u>Being underestimated could work to my advantage</u>. In those days, people didn't expect a short, young woman to come armed with research and good questions.

6. <u>I was an extrovert</u>. Joining a support group and an advocacy organization was therapeutic, for me. Withdrawing was not in my DNA.

7. <u>My inner voice was trustworthy</u>. Conventional wisdom isn't always wise, and often doesn't apply. No one else was in my shoes.

8. I was <u>stronger than I ever imagined</u>. While I had my moments, my priorities were clear — and all my important decisions took my brother into account.

9. I had a <u>decent brain</u>. In a very ambiguous, scary situation, I gathered a lot of information and thought for myself.

10. Despite a tendency to be gloomy and critical, <u>I loved life</u>. When I could laugh again, I knew I was going to make it.

Continuous Learning

Although I was often scared during the thirteen years after Michael's accident, I subconsciously used these twelve traits to forge ahead. As I entered new chapters of my life, I relied on these core strengths to navigate around new obstacles.

At 41, I had heart palpitations driving to work, having left my four-year old with my parents. Something was off, big-time. As a human resources director, I was weary of introducing management initiatives with magnificent overtures — only to see them fizzle out. I could detect a flavor-of-the-month deal by just watching an executive's body language. My sense of humor about organizational antics was severely strained.

So, after three years of stalling, I used my bias for action, and leapt into my own business, at 44. I don't know what my husband told them, but I later learned his family thought I had suffered a nervous breakdown: What woman in her right mind would walk away from a job with excellent pay and benefits?

I never felt freer. Until, of course, I had to pay quarterly taxes out of a shrinking bank account. But looking back, it was the right thing to do, for me.

****

At 61, I continue to question conventional wisdom. Despite a horrible economy and my advancing age, I am excited about making new things happen. And I still am awfully glad for my family, my health, my friends and my formidable mid-life brain.

In this economy, and our youth-oriented culture, finding sources of income and meaningful work is daunting. But I am determined not to flinch, and writing this book reflects those same traits and strengths I learned about myself so many years ago. Most importantly, I have friends to count on, and haven't lost my sense of humor. If anything, the absurdity of the present economy is freeing. With my shrinking time horizon, I am looking forward to exciting new developments — what's the worst thing that can happen?

Your Ten Terrific Traits

Think back to Chapter 5, as you were sketching out your Career Profile – past, present, and future. Force yourself to focus on positive aspects of your personality: What core traits have served you well to this point? What strengths have been honed through adversity and challenges? Write them down, now.

Make copies of this list and stash them in everyday places. Through repetition, you will update your mental software to include the wonder of you. Believe!

Focusing on traits at 55+ is especially important because, like friends, they are your secret weapons. What has helped get you this far will not abandon you. With your nimble brain, wealth of experience and wise insights, you can easily learn new skills and knowledge. Your essential characteristics provide the foundation for thinking positively about your next career move. What is your inner voice telling you? Be Bold. If not now, when?

~ My Ten Terrific Traits ~

1.

2.

3.

4.

5.

6.

7.

8.

9.

10.

Chapter 9. A Final Story: Miracles Do Happen

I think that wherever your journey takes you, there are new gods waiting there, with divine patience – and laughter.

Susan M. Watkins, Writer

Ignore mom's admonishment to never talk to strangers. We are all grownup now, and sometimes they bring us an important message. Most often, the courier is flesh and blood, but words may be whispered by no one at all.

Full disclosure: I believe in spirits. Around the time my consciousness was raised in the late '60s, I had an uncanny experience with a Ouija Board. Over these forty-plus years, I've sought counsel from psychics and read books by Sylvia Browne. Maybe because I am closer to a one-way ticket to the other side, my openness to all things unseen grows every year.

Whether you believe in angels, or chalk up unexpected events to gut instinct or good luck, you will enjoy this final story. "B," the main character, is short for Bernice, not Betty. But like the "Boop-oop-a-doop" character, she is full of fun. She also was a loyal wife, like Jerry's divorced ex-dancer. A Kansas native, her work ethic is unstoppable, like the beloved Betty White. She is also my mom.

B is a proud graduate of a Catholic girls' high school, and moved to California to start her working life. Her first job was for a company making contact lenses, which were new in the early '40s. One handsome patient was none other than Ronald Reagan, a well-known actor at the time. She remembers him as being especially polite and charming. B's astonishing beauty was in full bloom, and my guess is The Gipper was smitten.

B met and married her husband in Hollywood, then moved to be near his family in Connecticut when he was discharged from the Navy. At her urging, he turned down an offer as a chief mechanic with the Blue Angels. She was 25, pregnant with her second child (me), and wanted a grounded life.

Over her husband's objection, she went to work in an aircraft factory at age 28. He was a plumbing apprentice, and money was tight. His ego was hurt, but she was a realist.

B's work as a parts inspector was dirty; oil fumes burned away the hairs in her nose. She transferred to a clerical job in the finance department, which she said "a sixth-grader could have done." But the steady income and benefits were essential to the family, especially when her husband lost his superintendent job in their early 50s.

Around the time her husband started his own plumbing company, her pilot son was left totally disabled after crashing his plane. B was crushed, but soon after he was sentenced to a nursing facility, she brought him home. No one seemed equipped to care for a 28-year old man who could not make his needs known.

B mobilized a small medical unit in the winterized porch of their ranch house. She ordered supplies from the VA and hired home health aides for the work day. She learned how to care for her boy during the nights and weekends. Of course, people thought she had lost her mind to grief. Over a period of thirteen years, she proved them wrong. About mid-way, she took an early retirement, saying, "I feel like an old car that won't make it through another winter."

Six years after her son's death, and the joyous birth of her only grandchild, B flew to Las Vegas for a national plumber's convention. Laugh, but people who own plumbing companies do attend seminars and hold banquet dinners. A true worker-bee, she held a prominent position within the state Women's Auxiliary.

Then 70, B injured her knee rushing for a connecting plane on the trip out, and needed a place to sit while she waited for a workshop to start. Her husband suggested they try their luck at the nearby slot machines.

Fiscally conservative, B doesn't even buy lottery tickets. But she parked at the nearest machine and fed it quarters, one at a time. Her husband told her to double her bet, for God's sake: This was Quartermania. She only planned to spend $20, so why not?

Soon, a stranger spoke to her and motioned to the slot machine to her right. "Sit here, this is a lucky machine." He removed his credit card, smiled, and disappeared into the crowd. B shifted over.

Before B's $20 was spent, lights flashed and sirens screamed from that "lucky" machine. She was bewildered, and thought maybe she had broken

something. Um, no, she won the jackpot — $689,000!
Statistically, she had a better chance of being hit by
lightning, twice.

A deeply religious woman, B did not pray for money.
But on September 30th, which had been her father's
birthday, and was five days before the date of her son's
accident, she listened to a stranger. (And to her
husband – betting two quarters at a time produced a
much larger windfall.)

I'm not suggesting that every stranger you meet will
lead you to riches. But when we pay attention to our
surroundings and view the world as a friendly place,
we can make discoveries that refuel our resolve. It
may be a magazine article in a doctor's office, a TV
conversation you overhear on your way to doing
something else, or someone who asks for help.

Use your formidable mid-life brain to seize the day,
and own your life.

Bernice and buddies, ready to launch. 1944
(Bernice begged her dad to borrow his truck)

Chapter 10. Good Reads & 55+ Oath

Recommended Reading

I read to gain new perspectives, broaden my understanding of the world around me and escape from my daily demands. Some of the following titles are referenced in this book, and I also cite articles from two newspapers that I get home delivered. Many of these books include wonderful stories about friendships and growth. Hope you find something you enjoy.

Georgian

<u>If You Ask Me (And Of Course You Won't)</u>
by Betty White

<u>Here We Go Again</u> by Betty White

<u>The Secret Life of the Grown-Up Brain</u>
by Barbara Strauch

<u>The First Sex: The Natural Talents of Women And
How They Are Changing The World</u>
by Helen Fisher

<u>When Everything Changed: The Amazing Journey of
American Women from 1960 to the Present</u>
by Gail Collins

<u>My Stroke of Insight: A Brain Scientist's Personal
Journey</u> by Jill Bolte Taylor

<u>A Year by the Sea</u> by Joan Anderson

<u>Let's Take the Long Way Home</u> by Gail Caldwell

The New York Times

USA Today

ഇൗൃ

55+ Oath

Today I will use my ...

~ Nimble brain ~

~ Wealth of experience ~

~ Creative ideas ~

~ Wise insights and

~ Generous spirit ....

To help myself, and at least one friend, be a vibrant force in the workplace

ഇൗൃ

ABOUT THE AUTHOR

Georgian Lussier has 35 years of human resources and management experience. She earned a Master's Degree in Organizational Behavior in 1978 and is the author of two e-books on developing talent.

Born in 1950, she plans on working at least another fifteen years.

Visit her website, http://hrhelp.squarespace.com

10345767R00086

Made in the USA
Charleston, SC
27 November 2011